DEDICATION

These pages are dedicated to "The Fellows" who contributed to my growth and well-being as we played and grew up on and in the streets of Glenwood. We played football on dirt roads in front of our homes, basketball on dirt in the back yards with goals nailed to pine trees, and base/softball wherever we could.

In memory of some and much gratitude to those still with us, I dedicate this book:

George H. Hines, Jr.

Robert Alford

Bobby White

Earl Woodfaulk

Henry Hill

Gregory Woodfaulk

Ronald Woodfaulk

Willie Smiley

Alvin McNair

Willie Barnes

In every black neighborhood "back in the day" there were numerous groups of guys that spent more time together than they did at home. We were not unique, but uniquely fond of each other's company. This relationship gave all of us access to at least 3 or more moms who both chastised us and welcomed us into their homes all times of day and night.

Forward

By: George H. Hines, Jr.

I was honored when asked to write the forward for this book by my big brother, or should I say my older brother because I am bigger and taller than him! This picture book is a look back on what the Cove Boulevard corridor of the Glenwood section of Panama City, Bay County, Florida looked like in our youth.

We grew up in Glenwood in a neighborhood on 14th Street three blocks from Cove Boulevard now named M.L.K. (it runs from Business 98 to 23rd Street). Because the name Martin Luther King, Jr. Blvd. was not allowed to go into the affluent "Cove" neighborhood. The Panama City Mall delayed but eventually used the MLK address.

My older brother took out his camera and started recording what was left of the Black business store fronts in our neighborhood prior to the four-laning of Cove Boulevard, so that our history did not get completely lost. Myron K. Hines was born to Katie (Hobbs) Hines and George H. Hines, Sr. in Bay County, of Panama City, Florida. He grew up with three sisters and two brothers in the Glenwood section.

All the businesses and shops along Cove Boulevard were important to the people of this town because we were not really welcomed in the "other" part of town! Myron loves his hometown and never lived anywhere else for more than four months at a time. But our mother made sure that he and I went away almost every summer. We traveled to Texas, Kansas City, Georgia, Alabama, Oklahoma City and other places. He stayed in Panama City while both his brothers and one of his sisters went into the military. Both of his older sisters married military men and left Glenwood and Panama City. Myron had such a love for his community, he stayed here and took his time and skills to put together with his wife, Verma Bland Hines this picture book.

I can only hope that anyone that looks through the pages of this book remember what the Glenwood section of Panama City, Florida meant to black people and their families.

CITY DRUGS #2
533 N. Cove Blvd.

VALERIE TRUEBLOOD
615 N. Cove Blvd.

N. Cove Blvd.

GLENWOOD HISTORY
By
Ivie R. Burch

*(In the spirit of "Sankofa," an African term meaning
"looking back while moving forward," the Glenwood
Revitalization Project began with a series of oral
historical gatherings. Steering Committee historian Ivie
Burch facilitated the meetings, researched the
community's history and wrote an abridged history of
Glenwood.)*

The Glenwood Community has been referred to at varying
times by sundry groups as "The Quarters," as "East End,"
as "Shine Town," and some extremely negative
designations. It has existed since the nineteen-twenties;
and it has a noble history, with an incredible record of
perseverance and buoyancy. Like Bay County, it has been
populated by people from several areas of the country;
however, the turpentine, fish and sawmill industries as
well as tourism and stevedoring initiatives impacted the
growth of the population. All of the aforementioned
represented sources of livelihood for some of the early
settlers. There was, apparently, an innate desire by many
of these pioneers to become independent and mimic the
free enterprise system so common to this country by
becoming entrepreneur. Their efforts showed an unusual

amount of wisdom in that each business enterprise focused on the needs of a people in a segregated society of unequal financial opportunity.

This writing can, in its broadest sense, be referred to as an abridged history of Glenwood with regard to time frame and scope. The conversations and interviews of several significant community informers and the perusal of a limited number of historical sources have formed the nucleus of this look at Glenwood. The effort has been an attempt to present a microcosmic view of past economic and civic energies, which very well could challenge present day Glenwood residents to commit themselves to a spirit of revitalization.

POPULATION

The 1930 U. S. Census indicate that Bay County had a population of 12,091, and the population nearly doubled in the following decade to a population of 20,686 according to the 1940 census. The 1935 Panama City, Florida, Directory stated that the population of Panama City was 10,852 at the time of its publication. The motivations to locate in Bay County during the period 1930-1940 were increases in tourism and the Southern Craft Paper Mill, both providing increased job opportunities; hence, to assume that ten percent (10%) of the population in the decade 1930-1940 was non-white is, perhaps, a reliable assumption. The estimate of the black population in Bay County during the calendar year 1930 is 1,209, and the estimate of the black population in Panama City, Florida, during calendar year 1935 very well could be less than 1,000 people. This assumption is based upon the fact that the black population of the Bay County, Florida, census of 1930 included the residents of Bay Harbor, Lynn Haven, Millville, Youngstown, and Red Fish Point.

ECONOMICS

The economy of the Glenwood neighborhood in its infancy (1930-1950), as one would surmise, was influenced by multifaceted sources. All of the industries and many of the homesteads impacted the economic welfare of Glenwood residents in that some residents were domestic servants, some were found in the workplaces of the industry of the county, while others were self-employed. The name "The Quarters" indicated that many in the majority community viewed the residential area as the "quarters of their servants." Of course, there were many black persons who served as people who performed the chores in the homes of the more affluent residents. Other domestics were laundry women, yard men, chauffeurs, and handymen. Many of these persevering workers became the entrepreneurs of the Glenwood neighborhood. Pasco Gainer, Sr., the head bellhop at the Cove Hotel, became a renowned businessman. He had a successful rooming house, taxis, a funeral home, rental units, and a billiard polar (poolroom). His legacy is one which endowed his descendants with economic know-how and wisdom about common things. Malachi Crews, a stevedore, was a restaurateur in collaboration with his wife, Lucille Crews. Forsyth McClaren, a logger (forester), was a restaurateur.

MUTH & SONS PLUMBING
708 N. Cove Blvd.

HIDDLE HOUSE
Children's Shelter
707 N. Cove Blvd.

CLARENCE COLEMAN

712 N. Cove Blvd.

MARY L. BLOCKER
717 N. Cove Blvd.

Myron Hines

EDWARD & ANN SIMMONS

729 N. Cove Blvd.

PERFECTION DRY CLEANERS

Corner of 7th Ct. & N. Cove Blvd.

BLACK BUSINESS:1935 PANAMA CITY
DIRECTORY

Business	Type	Owner
Blue Front Café*	Rest.	James Dennis
Wells Café*	Rest.	J. W. Wells
Wells Barber Shop*	B-Shop	J. W. Wells
Sportsman's Inn*	N-Club	Ben Hunter
Davis Grocery*	Grc.	Wm. M. Davis
*East End		

Creature needs and a desire to exercise their unique skills in profitable ways gave rise to an enterprising group of businessmen and women many of whom preceded the entrepreneurs who came from the work force. While not listed in the 1935 directory, Lucille Crews, the wife of Malachi, operated a beauty salon adjacent to their restaurant which should have come into existence in this time frame. Rose Hunter Jackson operated a restaurant which reached its greatest popularity in the decade of the forties. Concurrently, she was the proprietor of a beauty salon which was adjacent to her restaurant.

BLACK OPERATED BEAUTY SALONS
1948 PANAMA CITY DIRECTORY

Mamie Burns' Beauty Shop	629 Harmon Ave.
Doralee's Beauty Shop	908 Mercedes Ave.
Lizzie Gautier's Beauty Shop	813 East 9th Court
Modern Beauty Shop	1014 Cove Blvd.
Queen of Beauty Salon	812 East 9th Court
Willie J. Ward's Beauty Shop	911 Louisiana Ave.

The beauty salon business flourished in the Glenwood area throughout its early decades of development, and, in terms of locale, these business endeavors were operational throughout the neighborhood. Dora Lee Crews, Mildred Cato, Lizzie Gautier, Addie Belle Everett, Lady Ethel Spires and others were competitive operators in their individual salons. Lady Ethel Spires was founder and operator of a vocational school for the teaching of the arts and skills associated with the industry. Several other operators were located throughout the area or as part of an established salon. The industry has survived uniquely in that beauty salons continue to be productive, and one school for the teaching of these arts and skills is located, presently, on Martin Luther King Jr., Boulevard.

Peter and Mama Lou Bryant were the owners of a rooming house at Harmon Avenue and Fifth Street prior to Pasco

Gainer entering into this phase of his entrepreneurship on the same site, and the Bryant's owned the property on Mercedes Avenue which became the initial site of St. John Baptist Church. Apparently, these people were very benevolent and had a real love for children as pointed out by Dora Lee Moses, a girl at the time that she knew them. In addition to the rooming houses previously discussed, Luvenia Holmes owned rooming houses on Harmon Avenue and Cove Boulevard. Her most recent business venture in this area was the Pamela Denise Motel which was demolished in the Martin Luther King Jr., Boulevard construction project. During this time frame, W. C. White, a teacher, owned and operated the Motel Neota which was located on North MacArthur. Joseph E. Lee, a pioneering law enforcement officer with the sheriff's department, continues to operate Lee's Motel on Martin Luther King Boulevard, a motel which lost only a small part of its structure to the restructuring project.

©2014 Myron Hines

BRYAN'S HOUSE OF BEAUTY

713 N. Cove Blvd.

MACEDONIA BAPTIST CHURCH

715 N. Cove Blvd.

PIONEERING BLACK CHURCHES

CHURCH	EST.	FIRST PASTOR
New Judson MB Church	1877	
Macedonia MB Church	1909	Rev. J. P. Glover
Greater Bethel AME Church	1910	Rev. L. D. Williams
St. John MB Church	1923	Rev. H. M. Hutchins
Holy Temple COGIC	1934	Rev. Robert L. McLeod
Tabernacle MB Church	1936	Rev. W. R. Walker
Mt. Olive MB Church	1943(sic)	Rev. W. S. Drayton
Gospel Temple FWB Church	1954	Rev. V. V. Barker
Mt. Zion PB Church	1944	Rev. P. L. Davis

The black church was a source of insight and strength in the development of the core of moral values and hope for the entire black community. Pivotal in these resourceful roles were the pastors of these churches whose guidance and encouragement gave many parishioners the courage to be all that God would have them be in rendering service to God and to their neighbors. Several of these pastors assumed major community leadership roles and were leaders in the organization of ministers known as the Ministerial Alliance.

Through substantiated testimonies, it was learned that the Ministerial Alliance was the most powerful, compelling entity for shaping community consensus and soliciting commitment from residents of Glenwood in a manner that was artful and somewhat subliminal. Its residual impact on the residents was absolutely mind boggling, so say those who were privileged to be participants in the meetings led by this group. This organization was composed of all of the pastors of black parishioners and the pulpiteers who were not pastors. The primary focus was spiritual with a secondary purpose of teaching residents to become full participant in the abundance of God's creation, which included the rights with which they were endowed by their Creator. Remembered for their leadership roles and outstanding participation are Pastors: Elijah Jones, R. L. McLeod, W. J. Johnson, Harold Long, Jr., Jackson E. Jones, W. R. Walker, Mickey Wills, Timothy Youngblood, P. L. Glover, Sr., and others. These Christian ministers formed an organization that was on one accord and spoke with one voice on the vast majority of issues. In the fourth Sunday community-wide meetings a superlative level of cohesiveness was displayed and communicated to the masses in the message of the speaker at that hour.

OUR LADY OF GRACE
Catholic Church
714 N. Cove Blvd.

THE FRONT PORCH BBQ
806 N. Cove Bvld.

STEPHEN'S WASH-A-TERIA

728 N. Cove Blvd.

MIRACLE DELIVERANCE CHURCH
816 N. Cove Blvd.

MRS. HARRIET MONER

824 N. Cove Blvd.

Corner of 9th St. & N. Cove Blvd.

Myron Hines

ANNIE B. WILKERSON
901 N. Cove Blvd.

900 Block N. Cove Blvd.

BLACK OWNED RESTAURANTS AND ENTERTAINMENT BUSINESSES: 1948 PANAMA CITY DIRECTORY

Hannah Blackshear	Tav*.	600 Harmon Ave.
Willie Conner	Café	573 Harmon Ave.
Harlem Bar & Café	Tav.*	----Cove Blvd.
Laulas Jackson	Café	531 Harmon Ave.
Little Savoy	Tav.*	908-10 Cove Blvd.
Lover's Rest Café	Café	1015 N. MacArthur
Lucille's Café	Café	828 Cove Blvd.
Old High Hat Café	Café	929 Cove Blvd.
Reno Bar & Grill	Tav.*	---- Harmon Ave.
Roosevelt's Café	Café	725 East 9th St.
Wayside Grill	Café	912 Cove Blvd.
Suwanee Night Club	Tav*.	1124 Varsity Dr.

Tavern*

This period of very pronounced lines of demarcation with regard to the races created a demand for creature needs in the area of adult entertainment and relaxation. Needs in this regard were met by the night spots such as the Sportsman's Inn, the Orange Blossom, the Reno Bar and Grill, the White Horse, the Old High Hat, the Little Savoy, the Harlem Bar & Café, Suwanee Night Club, and several minor night spots. These were not benevolent endeavors, for the proprietors of these businesses lived lucrative lifestyles. In addition, Pasco Gainer and Edward Benton offered leisure time activities in billiard parlors on Harmon Avenue and Cove Boulevard, respectfully. Quite noticeable among these establishments is that they were, for the most part, located along the main corridors, Harmon Avenue and Cove Boulevard.

STANLEY'S BARBERSHOP
Wayside Grill - Little Savoy
910 - 908 N. Cove Blvd.

J.C. WILSON SUBSTATION
corner of 9th Ct. & N. Cove Blvd.

WILSON BROS. BARBER SHOP
723E. 9th Court

© 2014 Myron Hines

CHARLIE'S TIME
913 N. Cove Blvd.

COMMUNITY STORE #1

928 N. Cove Blvd.

POOL ROOM-BAR

9th Ct. Behind Armstrong Grocery (928 N. Cove Blvd.)

BLACK OWNED GROCERY STORES
1948 PANAMA CITY DIRECTORY

Edward Benton's Grocery	---- Cove Blvd.
Blue Front Grocery	650 Wilson Ave.
J. R. Bowers' Grocery	1146 Cove Blvd.
Isaiah Cady's Gen. Mdse.	1016 MacArthur Ave.
East End Grocery	680 Harmon Ave.
W. R. Gautier's Grocery	1018 Cove Blvd.
Chas. Gaines Lincoln Pk. Super Mkt.	13th & Cove Blvd.
Tobe McCray's Grocery	944 Cove Blvd.
Fred Owen's Grocery	East 9th Street
Emanuel Pope's Grocery	908 East 10th
Wm. Sutton's Grocery	722 Hamilton

The benevolent element of the economic structure was associated with the grocery markets. The preponderant majority of the grocery markets provided some type of credit structure for the many residents who needed help in providing for their families. In addition to those listed above from the 1948 Panama City Directory, these stores included Lincoln Park Super Market, Sorey's Grocery on MacArthur Avenue, and Whit Everett's quasi grocery and variety store on Cove Boulevard. These stores provided easy access to the residents of the Glenwood neighborhood.

The concept of ethical behavior or business ethics was strongly embedded in the business choices of the Glenwood neighborhood. There was, apparently, a strong desire to render services that were worthy of the corresponding cost of such services. Such values gave rise to service-oriented businesses---full-service gasoline stations, laundromats, and dry cleaners. The decades of the forties and fifties saw a proliferation of such businesses— E. J. Brown's Grocery and Service Station, Ware's Union 76, McNeill's Shell, Robinson's Shell, Lee's Gulf Service, Anderson's Chevron, and Barnes Texaco for automotive services. Concurrently, the cleaning business saw the establishing of Jerry Masslieno's Monarch Cleaners, Tony Barnes Cleaners, Joe Barnes Cleaners, *Prows' Laundromat, Stephen's Laundromat, and Rhodes Laundromat. The vast majority of these businesses are extinct; however, a laundromat and two dry cleaning establishments are in existence on Martin Luther King Jr., Boulevard at the time of this writing, Fresh Scent and Barnes Dry Cleaners.

Perhaps, the arts and skills of many men in the Glenwood community provided the greatest hope and the greatest challenge for many of the Glenwood residents of yesteryears. Men of all sizes, ages, and temperaments were included among those noted for their skills, e.g., Dan Anderson, auto mechanic; Henry C. Bailey, carpenter;

Frank Comer, brick mason; Charlie Davis, carpenter; Albert Gary, carpenter and brick mason; Henry Gooden, carpenter; William Jones, carpenter and brick mason; Emanuel Jenkins and Cotes Jenkins, plaster-workers; Walter Ford, carpenter; Maxey Lawrence, carpenter; Frank Masslieno, cement finisher; Fred Oates, Sr. electrician; Morise Russ, Sr., shoe repairman; Henry Spears, carpenter; Walter Williams, carpenter; Ernest Woodruff, brick mason; and others who were not reported by community informers. Revisiting the arts and skills contributors to the economic development of the Glenwood community, the beauticians and barbers could be considered in this regard. Having listed significant contributors among beauty salons and their workers, it is quite appropriate to point out that the evolving of the barber shops in the community, from James Well to the present, has consisted of large and small shops governed by demand for service. The period of the Afro- Hair styles had a negative impact on the barbering industry. The Royal Barber Shop, located on East End, was a huge shop with colorful barbers in term of their unique personalities and their unique community roles; and it had a lively environment. Buddy Stanley's shop on Cove Boulevard (MLK) became the Wilson Brothers Barber Shop (Presently operating as an excellent shop), and Johnson's Barber Shop which existed until his demise.

though extinct, the black cab played a major socio.-economic role in the development of Glenwood. It provided transportation for black people to remote areas of the community which were not served by public transit vehicles, and it provided the opportunity for black people to avoid being told to go to the back of the bus; however, the "Shinetown" bus did not have the back of the bus stigma. The stigma was on the front of the bus, "Shinetown." The black cab or taxi business existed in the decade of the thirties. The testimony of a lady who arrived in Bay County in 1938 indicated she was picked up at the bus terminal by Bobby Weldon, a cab black driver. There was a minimum of two cab driver at this time, Bobby Weldon and W. R. "President" Gautier. Cab companies or associated groups had traditional names that, many times, defined their home base, i.e., East End Taxi, Royal Taxi, and Central Taxi.

HIS 'n' HERS HAIRCARE

944 N. Cove Blvd.

BARNES DRY CLEANERS

1003 N. Cove Blvd.

©2015 Myron Hines

WHITT EVERETTE
Whitt Everette Plumbing - Everette's Barber Shop
1030 N. Cove Blvd.

LEE'S GULF SERVICE STATION

1101 N. Cove Blvd.

Lee's Gulf Service Station which later changed to Lee's BP was owned by Edward Lee, Sr. This was a very successful business and allowed both blacks and whites to purchase fuel and associated supplies within the community.

Dan Lee says, "Each one of dad's four male children worked at the station from time to time. That allowed us to establish a firm community relationship and provided each of us with business skills."

The gasoline station was in full operation from 1958 to 1995. The widening of Cove Bouldvard (now MLK Bvld.) caused the station to permanently close.

Photo and Bio courtesy of Mr. Dan Lee

© 2014 Myron Hines

RUSS SHOE SHOP & SHOE REPAIR
1109 N. Cove Blvd.

Photo By: Myron Hines

RUSS SHOE SHOP AND STORE
1949-1999

After moving to Panama City Florida in late 1947 Morise and Clera opened Russ Shoe Shop at 1107 Cove Blvd. in 1949. Their shoe repair business was to become a pillar of the Glenwood community. About 1960, the Russ family built a new building next door at 1109 Cove Blvd. which included enough space to expand their business. Russ Shoe Shop and Store provided the Bay County residents another option for the purchase of shoes for their families. Over the next 30 years the business continued as a staple for the community with Morise and Clera Russ as active participants in the progressive development of Glenwood.

With the road widening of Cove/MLK Boulevard, the building had to be demolished and Clera decided to close the business since Morise was deceased and she was nearly 70 years young. They were very thankful to God for the provisions He had made for their family and the Greenwood community.

Dr. Muchere Russ

THE SHOP - AFTON'S HAIR DESIGN
1215 - 1217 N. Cove Blvd.

CIVIC/SOCIAL

Civic concerns of black people met the legal and illegal obstacles of the majority community and the civil government. This was really evident among black people who indicated that their interests were in enjoying the inalienable rights and the civil rights which were rightfully and legally theirs. Though the vast majority of the recorded information in this regard is oral history, many of those interviewed lived the experiences of this historic period. The period is historic and one worthy of note, for it represents the two decades (Forties and Fifties) in which the patience of many grew cold and the search for avenues to express to the city and county fathers the impatience which resided at the seat of their consciences, due to lack of governmental response, formed the focus of the agenda. In this environment the Negro Improvement Association was born. There were men who knew the powers that be and were strong God-fearing men committed to be all that they could be for their community. Included among these men were Pasco Gainer, Sr., Henry C. Bailey, W. J. Johnson, Rufus Wood, Sr., John R. Bowers, A. J. Ransom, R. V. Moore, Isaiah Thomas, C. C. Washington, and others. These men stood the proverbial "ten-feet tall" to persevere for the development of the infra-structure of the black community in total and Glenwood in particular. It was through the efforts of these men that lights, water and sewerage, and garbage services came to Glenwood. Roads were paved, and city and county law enforcement officers from the Glenwood area were hired and placed in the Glenwood neighborhood. Prior to their skillful application of what they had learned and observed, the city garbage dump remained on Cove Boulevard (MLK Jr Blvd.) between 12th Street and 13th Court and extended westward to Louisiana Avenue, and law enforcement was a farce with the sheriff's community "King Pin" having most of the clout. Remembered as the first city policemen who were black are James C. Wilson, Clyde McNeill and Howard "Buck" Steele; Remembered as the first deputy sheriffs who were black are Joseph E. Lee, Otis Wood and Freddy Clark.

In collaboration with the work of the Negro Improvement Association, a Women's Civic Club, composed of black women, worked diligently to bring about desired results in social-civic initiatives which complemented the efforts of the Negro Improvement Association. These women were under the leadership of Johnny Belle Murray and included Luella Washington, Irma Burford, Isabelle Drayton, Luvenia Holmes, Dora Lee Moses, Maudie M. Ransom and others. In a joint effort the two groups purchased the land on which the Martin Luther King Jr. Recreation Center was built. The organizations showed determination and self-control in following the essential steps to arrive at the present-day structure. Having procured the property, the land was deeded to the City of Panama City while Carl Gray was mayor, and the city built a small building without indoor plumbing, inadequate though a beginning. Through Dr. E. T. Buford's intervention, indoor plumbing was acquired. In 19– a new more adequate building was erected. Seemingly, the episode bears out the old adage; "If you do not care who gets credit for the task you can get the task done." Only the city officials are mentioned among those responsible for the existence of the center.

The Hospital Auxiliary, a task-oriented organization, of the fifties is highly revered by those who were members. Although the membership followed the doctrine of separation by race, which was viewed as an insult to the group's purpose, it was responsible for furnishing the segregated waiting area, for desegregating the hospital nursery, and engaged in many of the grounds enhancement projects. Remembering these experiences fondly are Luella Washington, Dora Lee Moses, Hattie Burch, Irma Burford, and others. Vestiges of this group seem to have been erased from the history of Bay Medical Center.

The decades of the forties and fifties gave rise to many bridge and social clubs which generated social and entertainment activities. In addition, these clubs gave the residents of the community the opportunity to define their peers in that club members were considered members of their social peer groups. Clubs adopted unique names for their fellowships, e.g. Egelloc (the reverse spelling of college), Jolly Seventeen, Queen of Hearts, and many others.

LINCOLN THEATER
1115 N. Cove Blvd.

BATTLE MEMORIAL FUNERAL HOME

1123 N. Cove Blvd.

Anderson's Service Station
was owned by
Willie and Bertha Anderson
and was open 6 days a week
from 1936 - 1986

© 2014 Myron Hines

ANDERSON'S STANDARD SERVICE STATION

1127 N. Cove Blvd.

ALFORD BARNES
1204 N. Cove Blvd.

GRADY'S ONE STOP DRIVE-IN RESTAURANT
1209 N. Cove Blvd.

ROBERT LEWIS, JR
1214 N. Cove Blvd

LUVENIA MITCHELL

1216 N. Cove Blvd.

FAITH TEMPLE
Church Of God In Christ
1224 N. Cove Blvd.

REV. W. H. WYNN

1226 N. Cove Blvd.

1228 N. Cove Blvd.

G. S. SIMMONS

1230 N. Cove Blvd.

CEMETERY

The Glenwood area continues to have one cemetery with a Warranty Deed dated January 19, 1916. Additional land was purchased June 20, 1940, by the trustees of the cemetery at that time. The agreement to purchase was signed by the officers of the board, i.e., Emmit B. Bush, Chairman; Henry Washington, Secretary; and C. H. Holmes, Treasurer.

EDUCATION

Education has always been the great emancipator for black people, and the struggle for unfettered opportunity to learn and be creative was a thirst in the early development of the neighborhood. The 1935 Panama City Directory lists Bella L. Hicks as principal of the Panama City Colored School. Also, Jenny Cooper and James Davis are listed as teachers in the Colored Schools. The Panama City High School which later became Rosenwald High School has a unique history of its own; however, it has been a practice in the field of education to sever or detach parts of schools in a system to meet needs as defined by the system. The high school had its lower grades severed to create a 1-6 elementary school, Glenwood Elementary School. This school was named A. D. Harris Elementary in 1968 by the Bay County School Board. Rosenwald High School was stretched in 1958 to become a junior/community college by adding on two additional grades, freshman and sophomore years of college. Oscar Patterson Elementary School was created by the Bay County School Board in 1954. The impact of the Glenwood community schools is awesome, having produced professional, scholars, and entrepreneurs in more fields than can be enumerated in this accounting. The schools in Glenwood had excellent leadership throughout their era of existence as black schools. Serving as principals in these schools, after the pioneering efforts of Bella L. Hicks, were James A. Grady, Richard V. Moore, Calvin C. Washington, Homer S. Jackson, Albert D. Harris, James Washington, Sr. and James Griffin.

EZELL'S CASH & CARRY MARKET
1247 N. Cove Blvd.

GRANT'S GROCERY & MARKET
1301 N. Cove Blvd.

DAN'S GARAGE

1309 N. Cove Blvd.

LADY ETHEL BEAUTY COLLEGE
1308 N. Cove Blvd.

REED PAINT & BODY - DOUGLAS KAR KARE

1354 - 1344 N. Cove Blvd.

GLENWOOD GROCERY
1409 N. Cove Blvd.

Frederick "Freddie" Clark - August 12, 1926 - August 14, 2009

Born in Florala, Alabama then moved to Panama City in 1934. Served for 7 seven years (1956 to 1963) as a deputy sheriff for the Bay County Sheriff's Department. Later in 1963, he became the owner and manager of the Glenwood Grocery Store and remained in business for over 35 years.
He loved old model cars, trucks, fishing and gardening. He was married to Bertha E. Kinsler Clark for fifty-four years. Their children include John, Bobby, and Terelyn Clark.

Photo of Mr. Clark & Bio provided by Bobby Clark

LEE'S MOTEL
1342 N. Cove Blvd.

Joseph E. Lee, originally from Redfish Point, Panama City Florida, was an outstanding businessman, Fishman, and father. His early career begin with him being drafted into the US Army. After serving four years, he returned to Panama City and got a job as a deputy sheriff from 1952 until 1965. His next adventure was as owner/operator of Lee's Motel. Joe Lee and daughters ran that business from July 1967 unil he sold it in 2004.

Photo and Bio courtesy of Lee Family

© 2014 Myron Hines

ECON-O-WASH SELF-SERVE LAUNDRY
Ralph Prows Superette Grocery
1425 -1427 N. Cove Blvd.

AFRICAN-AMERICAN CULTURAL CENTER
ORIGINALLY THE LITTLE PLAYHOUSE
14th Ct & N. Cove Blvd.

DAIRY DOME - CHURCH'S CHICKEN
Discount Auto Parts
1431 N. Cove Blvd.

ALL PROS SOLAR, LLC

1607 N. Cove Blvd.

GAINER FUNERAL HOME
24 Hour Ambulance Service
1613 N. Cove Boulevard

Mr. & Mrs. Harry & Geraldine Gainer

The Gainer Funeral Home was settled on Cove Blvd around 1951. The owners of the funeral home were Mr. Harry and Geraldine Gainer Sr. They served their community with love and compassion for over 45 years.
They had 7 children, Harry Jr, Gail, Tony, Gwendolyn, Terry, Sonya and Detra.
They left a well groomed legacy for their children.

Harry Gainer Jr. is now a certified license funeral director and embalmer.

Photos and Bio courtesy of Gainer Family

SPENCER GROCERY & MKT.

1617 N. Cove Blvd.

EMANUEL MACK

1713 N. Cove Blvd.

CONCLUSION

From everyone who has been given much, much will be demanded; and from the one who has been entrusted with much, much more will be asked. Luke 12:48b, NIV.

Glenwood, as defined by the Revitalization Committee, clearly communicates a history with several obstacles; however, it seems as if many of the significant players did not know they were operating under severe circumstances. They were not preoccupied with what was impossible. They were possibility thinkers and high achievers. Psychologists have given written data to indicate that the average person uses only 20 percent of one's brain, with only a persevering few individuals using more of their brain than the vast majority. These people who use more than 20 percent of their brain are call over achievers. Glenwood had an abundance of over achievers.

These pioneers were/are the real shakers and movers who dared to be successful and are the parents of Glenwood dwellers, including Generation X, a generation of people looking for the unknown term in the equation for effectiveness and prosperity. The history of Glenwood contains the solution to the equation and, therefore, the value for the unknown quantity, X. The answer seems to be twofold, challenge and opportunity, the ingredients which the pioneers used very effectively. The motivation to accept the challenge and opportunity to retrofit what once was alive and well, very well, could be the legacy that the significant players of the Glenwood history leaves this generation. This look back is filled with information which clearly indicates that many will help you thrive; however, those who reach superlative degrees of success do excellent things for themselves and their fellow humankind.

Ivie R. Burch